2012
The State of FEMA

Leaning forward:

Go Big, Go Early, Go Fast, Be Smart.

FEMA

Letter from W. Craig Fugate
FEMA Administrator

I am pleased to present "The State of FEMA: Leaning Forward; Go Big, Go Early, Go Fast, Be Smart." Since 1979, FEMA has worked collaboratively with our federal partners; state, local, tribal, and territorial officials; the private sector; non-profit and faith-based groups; and the general public to meet our mission. Thanks to the efforts of the whole community, we stand united and prepared to effectively meet the needs of our citizens during times of crisis – when they are most in need. This document is intended to highlight FEMA's guiding principles, the ways we are actively engaged with the emergency management community today, and the work we hope to accomplish in the future.

Being successful in emergency response means doing the homework and being equipped to respond to the largest scale disasters. It means being present early on the scene. It means operating swiftly, while also being smart. We at FEMA are doing that. And we're doing what it takes to do all of these things even better.

In 2011, FEMA responded to more disasters than any year in its history. The variety and magnitude of each event tested our capabilities, as well as the capabilities of communities across the country. While no one hopes to face the same volume of disasters in the coming years, it is imperative that we plan accordingly and continue to evaluate our strategic and operational approaches to serving the American public.

Moving forward in 2012, we will continue to focus on our strategic priorities. We will build on the progress made over the past two years and continue to foster a whole community approach to emergency management. With the completion of our all-hazards plans and National Disaster Recovery Framework, development of a National Mass Care Strategy, and implementing the FEMA Qualification System, we're strengthening the nation's capacity to respond to and recover from catastrophic events. Our strength will also come from our continued partnerships with tribal nations, the disability community, rural communities, and others. We have helped thousands of individuals and communities reduce the economic loss and human suffering associated with disasters by providing grants for mitigation activities. As part of Presidential Policy Directive 8, FEMA also led the effort to develop and publish a National Preparedness Goal – a national vision of preparedness and how the country will work together to approach our shared risks. Finally, we are improving the way we serve disaster survivors by enhancing our ability to improve and innovate based on lessons learned.

Projecting further, the Fiscal Year 2013 budget request focuses on achieving success in one of DHS' core missions: ensuring domestic resilience to disasters. As such, we place a strong emphasis on funding the key programs that help to ensure that as a nation we will effectively and rapidly respond to and recover from a variety of disasters.

Table of Contents

2011 Performance Highlights

FEMA responded to a record 98 major disaster declarations, 26 emergency declarations, and 112 fire management assistance grant (FMAG) declarations. Among those were tornadoes that devastated the town of Joplin, Missouri and severely impacted the southeast region, Hurricane Irene that impacted 35 million people along the east coast and record setting flooding in North Dakota.

FEMA established the Presidential Policy Directive 8 (PPD-8) Program Executive Office (PEO) to coordinate the implementation of PPD-8: National Preparedness with state, local and tribal leaders; federal partners; the private sector, non-governmental organizations, faith based and community organizations, and the general public. As part of the effort, the first edition of the National Preparedness Goal, which sets the vision for preparedness, was delivered to the White House.

FEMA released the National Disaster Recovery Framework which defines how federal agencies will work together to best meet the needs of states, tribes, and communities in their recovery, by aligning key roles and responsibilities among all our partners. FEMA is conducting town hall meetings around the country with our stakeholders to explain the framework.

FEMA provided approximately $2.9 billion (including Staffing for Adequate Fire & Emergency Response (SAFER) grants) in federal preparedness grants to assist states, territories, urban areas, federally recognized tribes, non-profit agencies, and the private sector in strengthening our nation's ability to prevent, protect, respond to, recover from, and mitigate all hazards.

In 2011 FEMA worked with stakeholders to conduct a comprehensive review of the National Flood Insurance Program (NFIP). By leveraging the expertise of our partners, FEMA believes this important effort will ensure that the program can more efficiently and effectively meet the needs of the public. The results of this analysis will inform decisions regarding the future of the NFIP.

FEMA helped train more than 428,000 individuals as part of the Community Emergency Response Teams (CERT) program. Overall, more than 1.3 million CERT volunteer hours were recorded in 2011. CERT teams in all 50 states responded to both small and large incidents providing local support to local citizens first.

FEMA supported the Great Central U.S. Shakeout, the largest-ever, multi-state earthquake drill in the United States, and the first major drill to take place along the New Madrid Seismic Zone (NMSZ). More than three million Americans across eleven states participated. Additionally, FEMA led the National Level Exercise 2011 which simulated the catastrophic impact of a major earthquake in the New Madrid Seismic Zone.

On November 9, 2011 the Emergency Alert System was tested nationally for the first time. The 30 second nation-wide test successfully identified areas of improvement to help strengthen our national emergency communication system. In all, millions of people experienced the test; the largest reach in the Alert's history. FEMA's Office of Disability Integration and Coordination, including our Regional Disability Integration Specialists, worked with the disability non-profit and advocacy community, especially the deaf and hard of hearing organizations, to spread awareness of the test.

Who We Are.

Since 1979, FEMA has been the federal government's lead agency in responding to and recovering from many of the nation's greatest moments of crisis. Throughout its history, FEMA has built upon more than 200 years of federal involvement in disasters. All told, FEMA employees have coordinated federal response and recovery efforts and supported state, local, tribal, and territorial efforts in more than 1,800 incidents.

We complete our mission as part of a team. We rely on our federal, state, local, tribal, and territorial government partners; the private sector; nongovernmental entities like faith-based and volunteer groups; and the public to deliver services and support to people in need.

FEMA's fundamental goal, and the inspiration and motivation for our FEMA employees, is to serve the nation by helping its people and first responders, especially when they are most in need.

FEMA is committed to the core values of compassion, fairness, integrity, and respect.

Compassion: Understanding and compassion do not only apply to FEMA's disaster work. FEMA personnel apply these values in dealing with co-workers, response partners, and non-disaster customers.

Fairness: FEMA's goal is that regardless of the outcome, all those with whom FEMA has dealings know that FEMA professionals listened to their concerns and treated them fairly and with respect.

Integrity: FEMA personnel recognize that integrity is their most valuable attribute and display their integrity by always conducting themselves honestly, dependably, credibly, and professionally.

Respect: FEMA employees are committed to treating those they serve and those with whom they work, with fairness, dignity, respect and compassion.

Our Guiding Principles

FEMA ensures that when communities rebuild after disasters they integrate the needs of persons with disabilities and others with access and functional needs into their community wide planning initiatives, and strengthen their ability to prepare for, protect against, respond to, recover from and mitigate all hazards.

Guiding principles direct FEMA's actions and are particularly important when the agency is faced with situations for which there is no clear direction. FEMA is committed to providing assistance and conducting all programs, services and disaster activity in a manner that includes the whole community and does not discriminate on the basis of race, national origin, color, religion, disability, age, sex, limited English proficiency, or economic status. For FEMA personnel, knowing and applying the guiding principles of teamwork, engagement, getting results, preparation, empowerment, flexibility, accountability, and stewardship helps to ensure that they consistently act in accordance with FEMA's core values.

Teamwork: FEMA employees are proud to be part of the nation's emergency management team and recognize that it is only through teamwork that FEMA can hope to accomplish its primary goal of supporting federal, state, local, tribal, and territorial government partners.

Engagement: Effective engagement means that FEMA employees respect and value the professionalism and capabilities that their partners provide and seek new opportunities and innovative ways to include partners in routine decision-making processes. This is in addition to their collaboration during the execution of disaster missions.

Getting Results: Getting results means identifying what must be achieved in terms of outcomes rather than processes. Understanding as clearly as possible what FEMA is trying to achieve improves the likelihood that FEMA personnel will make the best decisions under extreme pressure inherent during large-scale disasters.

Preparation: Preparation is the key to achieving the desired results. FEMA must continually plan, because the agency is guided by the mantra that failing to plan is planning to fail.

Empowerment: The nature of FEMA's responsibilities means that it must constantly lean forward and always be prepared to take decisive action. FEMA employees must be empowered to take actions expeditiously to achieve desired outcomes.

Flexibility: FEMA personnel work in dynamic environments characterized by rapidly changing priorities and ground rules. FEMA is prepared to adjust quickly as risks and stakeholder needs change.

Accountability: FEMA employees accept responsibility for accomplishing their missions, are transparent in their decision-making, and expect to be held accountable for the actions they take.

Stewardship: FEMA personnel are public servants entrusted with public resources to perform a critical mission. They have ethical, moral and legal responsibilities to protect these resources and ensure they are used effectively and for their intended purpose. FEMA employees are also entrusted with the responsibility to be good stewards of the nation's natural and cultural resources and take this responsibility very seriously in executing their mission.

The FEMA Culture

FEMA employee Susan Peterson conducts a FEMA for Kids Workshop at the Middleburgh Elementary School in N.Y. By participating in educational games and activities, students learn what to include in a disaster supply kit, how to protect pets during a disaster, and what their families can do during a disaster.

FEMA's fundamental goal, and the inspiration and motivation for many FEMA employees, is to serve the nation by helping its people and first responders, especially when they are most in need. FEMA's responsibilities further help to complement this ethos. Whether supporting state, local, tribal, and territorial governments in responding to and recovering from disasters, directly meeting the needs of disaster survivors, supporting the first responder community, or making the nation more resilient through preparedness or mitigation activities, FEMA employees have a unique opportunity and vital responsibility to help others.

The FEMA ethos also demands that FEMA employees help citizens and communities realize they have the power to help themselves. By focusing on this ethos, FEMA employees can make a real difference to the people and communities of this nation.

Preparedness: The preparedness mission seeks to reduce the loss of life and property and protect the nation by planning, training, exercising, evaluating and building the emergency management profession.

Prevention: The prevention mission seeks to avoid, prevent or stop a threatened or actual act of terrorism.

Protection: The protection mission seeks to protect our nation's constitutional form of government and ensures that a system is in place to warn our citizens of impending hazards.

Mitigation: The mitigation mission seeks to reduce or eliminate long-term risks to people and property from hazards and their effects.

Response: The response mission seeks to conduct emergency operations to save lives and property through positioning emergency equipment, personnel, and supplies; evacuating survivors; providing food, water, shelter, and medical care to those in need; and restoring critical public services.

Recovery: The recovery mission seeks to support communities in rebuilding so individuals, civic institutions, businesses, and governmental organizations can function on their own, return to normal life, and protect against future hazards.

By successfully executing these missions, we support our citizens and first responders to ensure that as a nation we work together to build, sustain, and improve our capability to prepare for, protect against, respond to, recover from, and mitigate all hazards.

Section I

Strategic Priorities

FEMA recognizes that we are only one member of a broad national emergency management team—one that includes federal, state, local, tribal, and territorial governments, the private sector, nongovernmental organizations, faith-based and community-based organizations, and the American public. Further, the agency acknowledges that the rapid pace of change in the world cannot be controlled and that the conditions we operate in will continue to evolve. At the same time, experience has taught us that we must do a better job of providing services for the entire community, regardless of their background, demographics, or challenges. This means planning for the actual makeup of a community, and making sure we meet the needs of every disaster survivor regardless of age, economics, or accessibility requirements.

Addressing these related concerns cannot be achieved by simply improving what we have always done – we must fundamentally change how we go about disaster preparedness, response, recovery and mitigation, involving the communities we serve directly in these efforts.

The "A Whole Community Approach to Emergency Management: Principles, Themes, and Pathways for Action" document is intended to promote a greater understanding of the FEMA approach and provide a strategic framework to guide all members of the emergency management community as they determine how to integrate Whole Community into their daily practices.

A lab technician prepares biological materials for use in future training at the Center for Domestic Preparedness (CDP). The CDP will begin using biological materials in training scenarios in 2012. Several key homeland security publications have identified the need for enhanced preparedness for biological attacks.

Foster a Whole Community Approach to Emergency Management Nationally

FEMA recognizes that it takes all aspects of a community (volunteer, faith, and community-based organizations, the private sector, and the public, including survivors themselves) – not just the government – to effectively prepare for, protect against, respond to, recover from, and mitigate against any disaster. It is therefore critical that we work together to enable communities to develop collective, mutually supporting local capabilities to withstand the potential initial impacts of these events, respond quickly, and recover in a way that sustains or improves the community's overall well-being.

Over the last two years, we have made significant progress in fostering a whole community approach to emergency management. Through the Maximum of Maximums initiative, national dialogue and outreach efforts, the whole community approach is now prevalent in the emergency management community. Across the country, we are seeing FEMA and our partners begin to exercise and implement the whole community approach and principles in their day-to-day activities.

The FEMA Mitigation and Insurance Strategic Plan for 2012–2013, embodies the concept of whole community engagement. The plan identifies specific goals, objectives, and strategies to help us better engage federal, state, tribal, territorial, and community partners in advancing mitigation activities. It embraces the reality that it takes all aspects of a community, not just the government, to truly reduce the devastating impact of disasters.

FEMA's Office of Disability and Integration Coordination and the Regional Disability Specialists have opened up the dialogue of making all programs and services accessible to all people with disabilities and those with access and functional needs. They have provided critical support to all levels of government.

FEMA has significantly boosted the level of interaction and collaboration with the broader private sector during disasters by launching a Private Sector Representative initiative in the National Response Coordination Center. To date, six companies have participated in 90-day rotations, including Target, Big Lots, Brookfield Properties, Verizon, Walmart and the first small business representative, from Strategic Planning Corporation.

To encourage a whole community approach at the state, local, tribal and territorial levels, FEMA wrote explicit language into the 2011 Homeland Security, Emergency Management, and tribal grant programs referencing the use of funds for private sector engagement. An accompanying private sector grant supplemental provides detailed ideas on how states might benefit from partnering with the private sector in emergency management and ways to use the funds to support successful efforts.

Mike Dayton (L) Acting Secretary of the California Emergency Management Agency (CalEMA) and David Ball (R) Disability Integration Specialist for FEMA Region 9 speak at the FEMA booth set up for the *Be Prepared!* emergency preparedness event hosted by CalEMA at the Capitol in Sacramento.

FEMA Region 10 partners with the FEMA Emergency Management Institute and the Boeing Company to conduct a four-day Integrated Emergency Management Course focused on a catastrophic flood event south of Seattle. More than 150 participants from five local communities, Boeing, and the State of Washington participated.

Shelter guests at the Hope Presbyterian Church in Memphis, Tenn. listen to information in Spanish from FEMA Region 4 translator Andres Lugo. FEMA supplies information in many languages.

In 2012, FEMA will:

- Leverage the Office of Disability and Integration and Coordination, Office of Equal Rights and Regional Disability Integration Specialists as part of the FEMA team working toward an inclusive model of emergency preparedness, response, and recovery.
- Continue to involve private sector representatives as part of the National Response Coordination Center to help engage private sector participation in emergency management, and develop plans to incorporate them into the Regional Response Coordination Centers.
- Expand and modernize the Integrated Public Alert and Warning System to include more Emergency Alert System Primary Entry Point Stations and the Commercial Mobile Alert System for delivering emergency alerts to cellular phones.
- Continue to strengthen partnerships with tribal nations, faith-based organizations, the disability community, rural communities and others.
- Exercise with partners to collaboratively prepare for hazards.

The 2013 request for increased funding in state and local programs for the National Preparedness Grant Program of $518,031 will allow grantees to develop and sustain core capabilities. Enhancing state and local capability further strengthens their communities and continues to foster a whole community approach.

Build the Nation's Capacity to Respond and Recover from a Catastrophic Event

During the last two years, we have instituted a forward leaning approach to "Go Big, Go Early, Go Fast, Be Smart" by focusing on "Maximum-of-Maximums" planning. Key benchmarks for FEMA's response and recovery resulting from a catastrophic event are to stabilize the event to meet the needs of survivors within 72 hours, restore basic services and community functionality within 60 days, and return communities to normalcy within five years. The critical outcomes for 14 Response and eight Recovery Core Capabilities have been quantified and incorporated into the National Preparedness Goal to be implemented through national and regional plans.

In 2012, FEMA will:

- Develop an all-hazard Federal Interagency Operational Plan in conformance with the new National Preparedness Goal.
- Develop all-hazard operational plans for each of the ten FEMA Regions, including incident-specific annexes for unique catastrophic situations.
- Develop a National Mass Care Strategy.
- Implement the Crisis Management System to improve understanding of the common operating picture.

Only one hurricane hit the U.S. in 2011 but it affected 14 states and more than an estimated 35 million people. Hurricane Irene left her mark all along the east coast, but the non-coastal state of Vermont suffered flooding that amounted to the state's worst disaster ever. FEMA pre-positioned commodities and people in all 14 states, enhancing communications efforts and speeding response.

Jason McNamara, Chief of Staff for FEMA, discusses the new Workforce Transformation initiative and FEMA Qualification System with Region 7 employees. All ten of the FEMA regional offices hosted similar events to educate and inform the workforce of these changes.

Region 2 FEMA representatives thank Home Depot store manager as he and other employees are honored with a Certificate of Appreciation for their role with hosting community education and outreach events in the wake of Tropical Hurricane's last year.

- Implement the FEMA Qualification System to strengthen workforce operations and enhance the reservist program through the disaster workforce transformation.
- Develop stronger government-to-government relationships with tribal nations.
- Build out the components of the National Preparedness System and the associated National Planning Frameworks and Federal Interagency Operational Plans for each mission area, the National Training and Education System, and the National Preparedness Report.
- Foster a culture of preparedness across the whole community through a campaign to build and sustain preparedness.
- Enhance monitoring capabilities for radiological and nuclear incidents to rapidly inform consequence management activities.
- Conduct modeling and analysis to inform critical decision making and facilitate rapid incident stabilization during a catastrophic incident for the Institute for Business and Home Safety and others and enable the agency to effectively message communities and states to adopt and enforce building codes to create more disaster-resilient and sustainable communities including compliance to Americans with Disabilities Act (ADA) and federal laws to make communities accessible for all.

Build Unity of Effort and Common Strategic Understanding

The nation must manage risk and prepare for, protect against, respond to, recover from, and mitigate against the impacts/consequences of risks to the health and welfare of the American people. It is essential to develop a common understanding of the risk landscape to identify mitigation and prevention opportunities across all mission areas, estimate required resources, assess gaps, build and sustain capabilities, and plan to deliver them. Risk based planning is about understanding the broader risk landscape/picture from key perspectives (state, region, national).

As part of the implementation of Presidential Policy Directive 8 (PPD-8), FEMA released of the first-ever National Preparedness Goal. The Goal identifies the core capabilities and capability targets necessary to advance our national preparedness. It builds extensively on the prior work of many stakeholder groups from around the nation, draws upon lessons learned from large-scale and catastrophic events, and represents input from all stakeholders. It also recognizes that as we work to build a more prepared nation, we cannot only look at the role that government plays, we must also work with the entire community – both the public and private sectors, faith-based and non-profit organizations, and most importantly the public.

Members of AmeriCorps New Jersey team pack and assemble health and hygiene kits for distribution to disaster survivors. AmeriCorps is one of many organizations who provide assistance to disaster survivors through the coordinating efforts of FEMA.

"I don't think there is much to mumble and grumble about...Everybody feels secure about getting help."

Alabama Resident
Axavier Wilson
New York Time
May 1, 2011

In 2012, FEMA will:

- Conduct second generation Regional Threat and Hazard Assessments to improve and refine understanding of our nation's greatest risks to provide a solid risk-based foundation for preparedness and planning efforts.
- With the National Preparedness Goal complete, continue to work on additional requirements of PPD-8:
  - A National Preparedness System Description.
  - A series of National Frameworks and Federal Interagency Operational Plans.
  - A National Preparedness Report.
  - A campaign to build and sustain preparedness

Enhance FEMA's ability to learn and innovate

Operational realities have taught us that no matter how much we prepare, it is still impossible to predict exactly what will happen in a disaster environment. FEMA's initiative to enhance our ability to learn and innovate puts a premium on developing organizational capacity to learn from past experience, rapidly orient and apply that learning in current contexts, and adapt to quickly changing conditions. FEMA can facilitate organizational growth by improving its evaluation of operational performance in both real world incidents and simulated exercises, and sharing lessons learned best practices, and corrective actions following events and exercises throughout the whole community.

In 2012, FEMA will:

- Begin a multi-year effort, working with FEMA's partners, to update and enhance the software and procedures that support tracking corrective actions and sharing lessons learned through systems like the Lessons Learned Information Sharing Systems (LLIS.gov).
- Implement a performance-based FEMA Qualification System for 23 cadres and 322 disaster positions.
- Continue implementing the FEMA Future Leaders program.
- Continue implementation of the FEMA Stat Program.

Georgia local officials, SBA, and FEMA work together to conduct Preliminary Damage Assessments (PDA) to determine the extent and magnitude of damage after severe storms and flooding affected the area.

Signatures and messages of hope from thousands of volunteers are written on the walls of this home damaged by the tornado that hit Joplin, Mo. in May 2011.

CASE STUDY: Center for Domestic Preparedness (CDP) Training Vital to North Dakota Flood Response

As Bill Brown received flood condition updates in June 2011, city officials in Minot, N.D. were preparing for the worst overflow in more than 130 years. Brown, a retired captain with the Minot Police Department and now the Southwest Regional Emergency Response Coordinator for the North Dakota Department of Emergency Services, was making arrangements to staff the city's Emergency Operations Center and coordinate state resources to assist in the flood response.

Brown, a veteran of 19 courses at the Center for Domestic Preparedness, has trained in a variety of subjects to include law enforcement protective measures and response to a mass casualty event involving Weapons of Mass Destruction. However, during this event, it was not terrorists or domestic criminals threatening the streets of Minot, it was water—a lot of water. More than ten feet of water from rivers surrounding Minot and other North Dakota communities poured through the streets, sweeping homes and store fronts away and forcing the evacuation of more than 12,000 people.

Bill Brown, North Dakota Department of Emergency Services, attributes his CDP training to his successful response serving in the logistics department of the Region 8 Minot, N.D. Emergency Operations Center.

"I found the course of instruction at the CDP to be more of a real-world scenario allowing me to better retain the information," Brown said. "The Incident Command System class gave me the opportunity to better understand the roles of each division within the incident command structure as well as understanding the diverse perspectives of different responder disciplines. Having had this training allowed me to have a more effective understanding and better line of communication with the private, local, state, and federal organizations."

Section II

FEMA Programs and Missions

FEMA's mission is to support our citizens and first responders to ensure that as a nation we work together to build, sustain, and improve our capability to prepare for, protect against, respond to, recover from, and mitigate all hazards. In carrying out that mission, FEMA employs a dedicated workforce of full time staff and reservists who focus on making sure that the nation is prepared and that our efforts to assist during times of crisis are a priority.

"In the wake of last Wednesday's severe storms and tornadoes, FEMA has reacted – in bureaucratic speed anyway – lightning fast."

Birmingham News
Editorial Board
May 4, 2011

The Office of Response and Recovery provides leadership to build, sustain, and improve the coordination and delivery of support to citizens and state, local, tribal and territorial governments to save lives, reduce suffering, protect property and recover from all hazards.

Response and Recovery

"The Administration's response to Hurricane Irene has been great; there are already FEMA first responders on the ground coordinating with local first responders, and they're doing a great job with response and recovery efforts."

Delaware Governor
Jack Markell
MSNBC
August 27, 2011

In 2011, FEMA brought the Response, Recovery and Logistics Management Directorates together in the Office of the Associate Administrator for Response and Recovery (ORR) in order to better align their complementary missions. The ORR oversees all gubernatorial requests for emergency declarations and major disasters declared by the President in compliance with the Robert T. Stafford Disaster Relief and Emergency Assistance Act.

The ORR also provides strategic level coordination, leads resource integration, and oversees FEMA's major operational components. These include the Response Directorate, the Recovery Directorate, the Logistics Management Directorate, the Office of Readiness and Assessment, and the Office of Federal Coordinating Officer.

Response

In 2011, FEMA's Response Directorate provided the federal operational capabilities needed to save lives and support survivors in a record number of communities overwhelmed by natural disasters. The Response Directorate also undertook efforts that will strengthen the capabilities and readiness of FEMA's response teams and personnel, improve tactical emergency communications during disasters, and establish doctrines and plans to ensure FEMA effectively engages with emergency management partners from across the whole community.

After Hurricane Irene hit the state, Region 1 employees work in FEMA's Mobile Emergency Response Support/Systems vehicle at FEMA's Initial Operating Facility at the Emergency Operations Center set up in Hartford, Conn.

"We want to thank them for being 'Johnny on the spot' from the beginning."

Birmingham, Ala. Mayor
William Bell
AP, May 2, 2011

Response 2011 accomplishments include:

- Preparing for and responding to a record 98 major disaster declarations, 26 emergency declarations, and 112 Fire Management Assistance Grant (FMAG) declarations, including:
  - Major spring floods that caused historic flooding in parts of the mid-south;
  - Historic fire season that burned more than 7.8 million acres of wild lands;
  - Devastating severe storms that spawned tornadoes and thunderstorms from Arkansas to Illinois to New England;
  - Dynamic hurricane season, including Hurricane Irene and Tropical Storm Lee for which we leveraged our authorities and plans to strategically prepare and respond:
    - Made federal resources available to states in advance of and following the storm, including commodities such as water, meals, and tarps.
    - Imbedded 14 Incident Management Assistance Teams and other FEMA liaisons in 14 states to assist with preparations, evacuation support, and response operations.
    - Activated major federal assets, such as national Urban Search and Rescue (US&R) teams that performed search and rescue operations in at least three affected states.
    - Positioned critical communications assets, like FEMA's Mobile Emergency Response Support capabilities, along the east coast.
    - Deployed more than 4,000 reservists for a total of more than 6,000 FEMA personnel, in support of response and recovery efforts.
- Coordinated and participated in National Level Exercise 2011, which brought together federal, state, local, tribal and territorial partners to simulate a whole community response to the impacts of a catastrophic earthquake in the central United States.
- Led initial development efforts for a Federal Interagency All-Hazards Response Plan and scenario-specific annexes that integrate prior planning efforts, including non-traditional response strategies required for catastrophic disasters.
- Established and piloted the DHS Surge Capacity Force (SCF) in partnership with the Transportation Security Administration (TSA) and U.S. Customs and Immigration Services (USCIS); the SCF draws upon DHS' diverse workforce to provide just-in-time training to surge staff to fill operational gaps during disasters.
- Continued coordination efforts among the Emergency Support Function Leadership Group (ESFLG), the senior level entity that coordinates responsibilities, resolves operational and preparedness issues, and provides planning guidance and oversight for interagency response activities.

FEMA Region 4 Community Relations Specialists speak with a storm survivor in front of her former home in Phil Campbell, Ala.

During a Joint Field Office visit, Federal Coordinating Officer Kevin Hannes shows Bill Carwile, FEMA Associate Administrator for Response and Recovery and Deborah Ingram, FEMA Assistant Administrator for Recovery, a Texas map depicting the areas affected by the devastating wildfires.

"This story is really about the donated resources – about everyone coming to help us. Not only have they helped us clean up our community but they have helped us financially, in the fact that, if we would have had to pay our share from this entire disaster, it would have taken us a lot longer to recover."

Leslie Jones
Director of Finance, City of Joplin
KYTV Springfield, Mo.
January 18, 2012

David Myers, director of the DHS Center for Faith-based and Neighborhood Partnerships talks with NYU student volunteers. Jewish and Muslim NYU students volunteered at a job site where two new homes were built in Pratt City, Ala. FEMA funding and coordination with volunteer agencies helped make that happen.

Recovery

In 2011, FEMA obligated $4.7 billion in assistance, primarily for Individual Assistance (including housing, crisis counseling, legal services, disaster case management, and unemployment assistance, among other services) and Public Assistance (including reimbursement to clear debris and rebuild roads, schools, libraries, and other public facilities).

In the wake of deadly tornadoes that devastated the south and midwest in the spring of 2011, FEMA worked aggressively to support the impacted communities and the survivors in their desire to build back safer through a series of initiatives to promote safe rooms and public and private facilities throughout the impacted regions. The team brought together building science engineers, grant, communication and environmental specialists, and emergency managers to work with partners at the state and local levels, launching an awareness campaign on the benefit of Safe Rooms, conducting a forensic analysis of damages that would inform the recovery and by streamlining the environmental review and grant application processes that will ultimately make it easier for communities and individuals to apply and qualify for mitigation grants for safe rooms and community shelters. Through their unity of effort FEMA's Recovery Directorate and Federal Insurance and Mitigation Administration demonstrated what can be accomplished when all are dedicated to the purpose of building back strong.

Recovery 2011 accomplishments include:

- Released the National Disaster Recovery Framework (NDRF) which was developed in partnership with stakeholders representing local, state, tribal, territorial, and federal governments, private organizations, professional associations, academic experts, and communities recovering from disasters. The NDRF defines how federal agencies will work together to best meet the needs of states and communities in their ongoing recovery, by aligning key roles and responsibilities among all our partners. To date, forums and training activities have been conducted nationwide with more than 1,300 participants from the whole community, including representatives from federal agencies, states, tribes, local government, non-governmental organizations, and the private sector. Additional forums in six cities are planned throughout February and March.
- Implemented a new initiative (Operation Clean Sweep/Expedited Debris Removal) to expedite removal of debris after the severe tornado disasters in Alabama, Mississippi and Missouri. FEMA worked with the states and localities to expedite authorizations of private property debris removal and rights of entry in the hardest-hit areas to help get people back into their homes. Total amount of debris removed in Operation Clean Sweep/Expedited Debris Removal was 6.5 million cubic yards in Alabama, Mississippi and Missouri.

FEMA Community Relations Specialist explains the FEMA registration process at the Iglesia Metodista San Juan church in Clanton, Ala. FEMA is supporting the recovery from the severe storms, tornadoes, straight-line winds, and flooding that damaged or destroyed parts of Alabama during the period of January 22-23, 2012.

- Conducted four Recovery events as part of National Level Exercise 2011 including: A National Recovery Seminar, State Recovery Transition Discussions, State Recovery Workshops/Tabletop Exercises, and the National Recovery Tabletop Exercise.
- Developed the Disaster Case Management Program Manual to be used by regions and states in the development, implementation, and delivery of ongoing case management services for connecting disaster survivors with local providers that can target recovery services to assist them in developing and achieving short and long-term recovery goals. In 2011 more than 14,255 disaster survivors benefitted from the implementation of this program in eight disasters nationwide.
- Developed capability within the National Processing Service Center to provide outgoing email to disaster survivors allowing for immediate online access to eligibility determinations. Since August, over 108,000 disaster survivors have accessed their eligibility determinations online.
- Established the National Mass Care Council, co-chaired by the American Red Cross and National Voluntary Organizations Active in Disasters to promote development of a National Mass Care Strategy and provide a framework to enhance coordination, pool expertise, and build the national mass care capacity engaging the whole community, including people with access and functional needs.

CASESTUDY:
Getting Back to School in Joplin, Mo.

Just days after the tornado ripped through Joplin, the date of August 17 became a goal for measuring progress on the recovery of the community. That date was the start of the next school year, and for returning high school students it would also mean learning in a new place. Getting school started on time was also a community rallying point. So the community went to work. A temporary high school facility was located and leased, and volunteers and faith based organizations kicked in by painting rooms and hallways, assembling furniture, and setting up classrooms. Private donations – a $1 million dollar donation from the United Arab Emirates– funded computers and provided books and supplies. FEMA along with state, federal and local government provided funding and guidance. On a city-wide level, Joplin's Citizen Advisory Recovery Team, comprised of many local organizations, led the effort to develop community plans to bring Joplin back to normal. Joplin is a community coming together and its high school, rising from the debris, has a new look and can-do attitude.

Individuals and Households Program Funding Amount
Per County During 2011

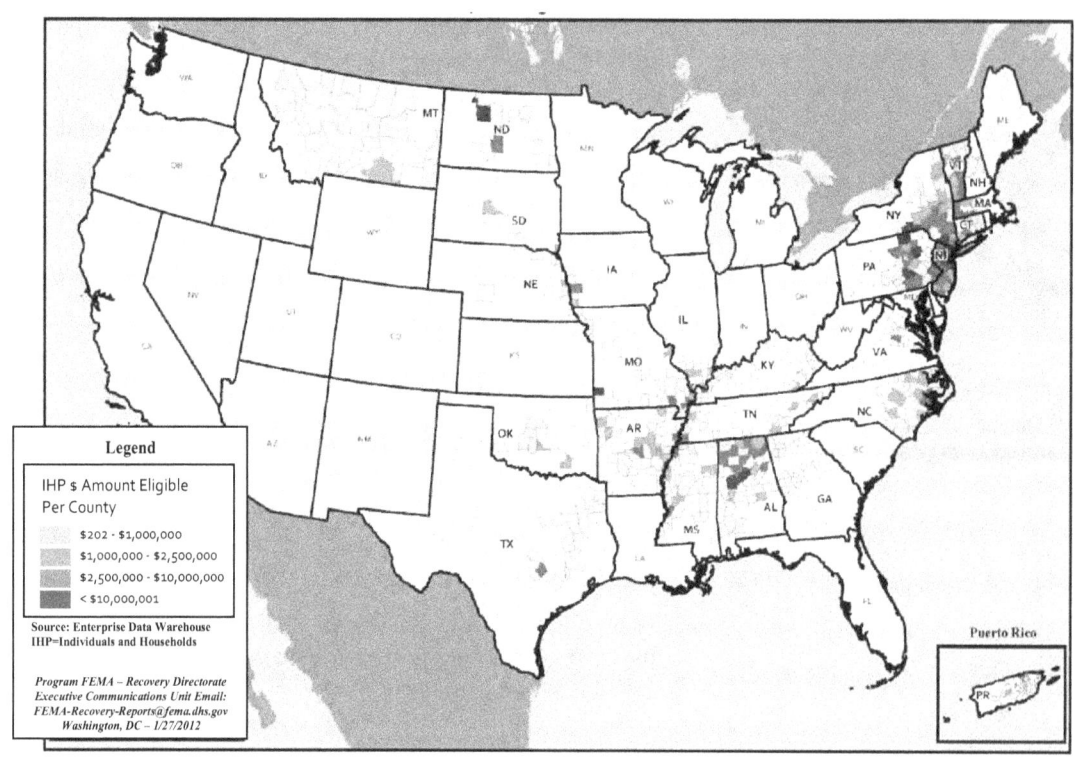

Public Assistance – Total Funding Obligated
Per County During 2011

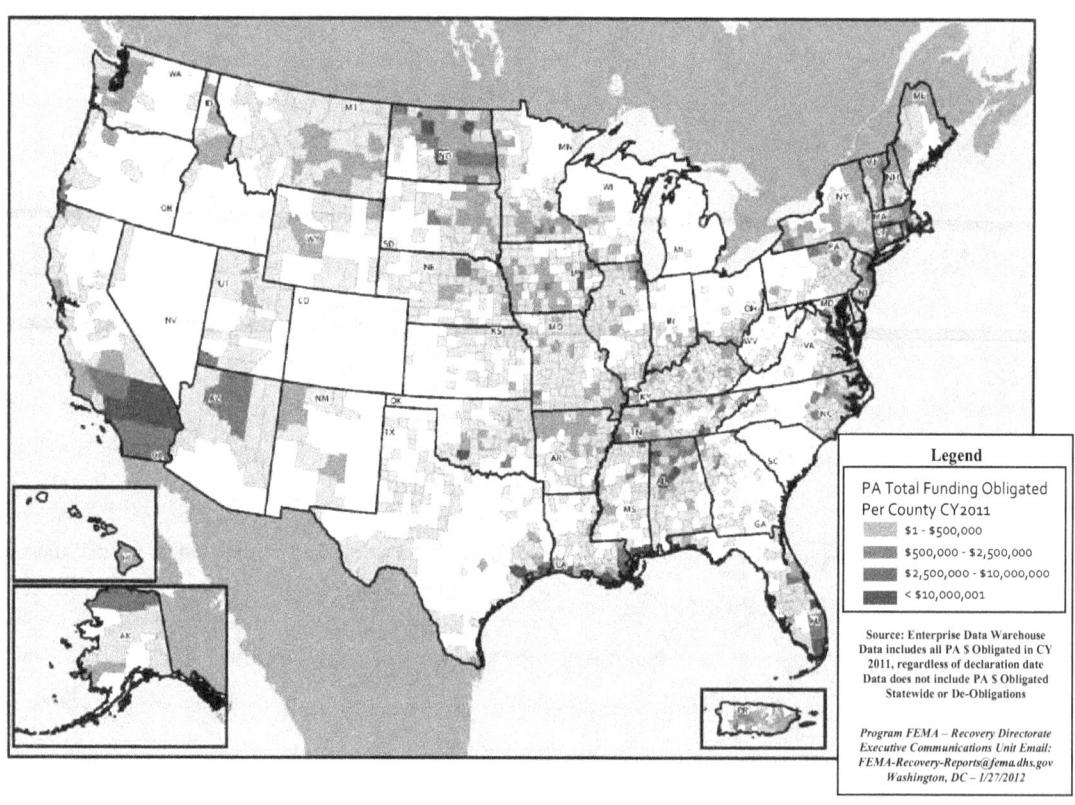

Region 6 logistics teams at the staging area in Camp Beauregard La., load CUSI Kits (Commonly Used Shelter Items) now part of the commodities to be delivered to the shelters in the event of a disaster.

On a scale of one to 10, they are a 12... I think they (FEMA) are doing an excellent job.

Missouri Congressman Billy Long
Springfield News-Leader.com
May 30, 2011

Region 5 logistics staff sorting supplies staged at the Incident Support Base in Arden Hills, Minn. Staging of materials in case of flooding in a multi-state area of the midwest.

Logistics

FEMA's Logistics Management Division serves as the National Logistics Coordinator and single integrator for strategic logistics planning support and coordinates all domestic emergency logistics management and sustainment capabilities. The Directorate is responsible for policy guidance, standards, execution, and governance of logistics support, services, and operations. FEMA Logistics co-leads Emergency Support Function #7 (Logistics Management and Resource Support) with the General Services Administration.

Logistics 2011 accomplishments include:

- In response to a record number of disasters affecting 47 states, including Hurricane Irene, Tropical Storm Lee and multiple tornadoes, floods and severe weather throughout the U.S., FEMA and our interagency partners delivered over 24 million meals, almost 12 million liters of water, thousands of cots, blankets and tarps, infant and toddler kits, durable and consumable medical equipment and over 4,000 temporary housing units to disaster survivors.
- FEMA and the General Services Administration collaborated with the United States Army Logistics University to deliver four Interagency Logistics Courses. The purpose of the course is to familiarize students with logistics planning considerations and the role of the interagency in disaster relief and humanitarian assistance missions.
- Completed the build-out of the new Atlanta Distribution Center facility located near the Hartsfield-Jackson Airport in Atlanta, Georgia. The facility includes approximately 407,000 square feet of warehouse/office space situated on 31 acres.
- Expanded efforts to better assist federal, state, local, tribal, and territorial partners in meeting the needs of children, infants, the elderly, and people with disabilities and those with access and functional needs, by providing baby food and infant formula, children and elderly specialty commercial meals, durable medical equipment, consumable medical supplies, and functional needs cots.
- Completed the final disposal of over 120,000 excess Temporary Housing Units, including Katrina era units and more recent units returning from Hurricane Ike. All 21 original disposal sites have been closed, resulting in approximately $35 million in operations cost avoidance.
- Completed more than 93 percent of orders for required life-sustaining commodities (meals, water, tarps, plastic sheeting, cots, blankets and generators) and key operational resources in support of disasters within the agreed-upon delivery date.
- Conducted and/or provided oversight of 100-percent inventories of all distribution centers and temporary housing staging areas and achieved a 99-percent annual reconciliation accuracy of disaster response supply inventory.

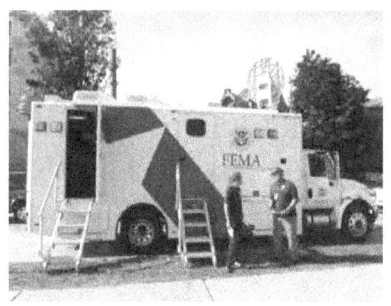

FEMA Region 1 Community Relations Specialists discuss outreach strategy. They were deployed in support of recovery efforts following the heavy rains and flooding that accompanied Tropical Storm Irene, which struck the state of Vermont on Aug. 28, causing extensive damage. Community Relations Specialists are responsible for providing information to the public and gathering information from the field as part of FEMA's response.

"FEMA is doing a great job of getting the information out there on how victims can get in touch with FEMA."

Tornado survivor Christie Greky
NBC Nightly News
May 3, 2011

Region 3 Angela D. Green, FEMA Quality Assurance/Quality Control Specialist for the Centralized Processing Center earned The Bronze Star Medal for meritorious service in Afghanistan. Dan Smyser, FEMA Public Assistance Group Supervisor presented the medal to Staff Sergeant Angela Green in the presence of family, friends and co-workers.

Readiness and Assessment

The Office of Readiness and Assessment was established in late in 2010 and became fully operational in mid 2011. It enables the FEMA Administrator and agency leaders of reporting organizations to uniformly determine and accurately report an overall level of readiness by FEMA to fulfill its disaster response, recovery, and logistics missions.

Readiness and Assessment 2011 accomplishments include:

- Developed evaluation processes for regional offices, Mobile Emergency Response Support (MERS) and distribution centers.
- Facilitated Hurricane Earl and winter storm "hot wash" operational reviews and developed "Quick Look" reports of operational findings. Several findings from the operations reviews were incorporated into and enhanced our response to Hurricane Irene and Tropical Storm Lee. These enhancements included cross-regional IMAT support & resource prioritization.
- Conducted pilot evaluations of the readiness of two MERS detachments. Key operational findings and recommendations for enhancement are being addressed by MERS leadership. These include identification of need for improved HQ/Detachment communication, detachment staffing, and standard operating procedures.
- Conducted evaluation visits to eight regions and identified cross-agency issues pertaining to Regional Response Coordination Centers (RRCC), IMATs, watch operations and vehicle distribution.
- Provided operational analysis support to the Alabama Joint Field Office (JFO) resulting in a project plan to support the Federal Coordinating Officer's (FCO) JFO management and efficiency targets.

Senior officials discuss response operations to the massive winter storm affecting a large part of the nation during a video teleconference with regional and federal partners at FEMA's National Response Coordination Center.

Protection and National Preparedness (PNP) is responsible for the coordination of preparedness and protection related activities throughout FEMA, including preparedness grant programs, planning, training, exercises, individual and community preparedness, assessments, lessons learned, continuity, and national capital region coordination.

Protection and National Preparedness

"We can't control when or where a terrible storm may strike...but we can control how we respond to it."

President Barack Obama
New York Times
May 1, 2011

State and Local Preparedness

In 2011, FEMA awarded approximately $2.9 billion (includes SAFER grants) in homeland security grants to assist states, territories, urban areas, federally recognized tribes, non-profit agencies, and private sector entities in strengthening our nation's ability to prevent, protect, respond to, recover from, and mitigate terrorist attacks, major disasters and other hazards.

In 2011, FEMA obligated:

- 56 State Homeland Security grants, totaling $526.8 million
- 31 Urban Areas Security Initiative grants, totaling $662.6 million
- 21 Urban Areas Security Initiative Nonprofit Security grants, totaling $18.9 million
- 58 Emergency Management Performance grants, totaling $329 million
- 26 Emergency Operations Center grants, totaling $14.6 million
- 48 Driver's License Security grants, totaling $73.7 million
- 123 Port Security grants, totaling $235 million
- 39 Transportation Security grants, including 7 Freight Rail Security grants, totaling $200 million
- 1 Intercity Passenger Rail Security grant, totaling $22.2 million
- 10 Regional Catastrophic Preparedness grants, totaling $14 million
- 83 Intercity Bus Security grants, totaling $4.99 million
- 3,554 grants to fire departments throughout the United States, totaling $775.9 million
- 21 Tribal Homeland Security grants, totaling $10 million

Over $5 billion in grant funds were dedicated across grant programs to reinforce specialized first responder teams through measures such as bomb squad trainings, exercises, and equipment purchases, including tactical robots, x-ray imaging systems, response vehicles, explosive ordinance disposal K-9 teams, communication systems and protective clothing. Today, there are over 460 bomb squads equipped, trained and ready.

Amtrak used Intercity Passenger Rail (IPR) funding to build detection and prevention capabilities against the threat of Improvised Explosive Devices (IEDs). IPR investments served as a force multiplier, helping Amtrak increase the number of K-9 detection teams nationwide from 10 in 2005 to 52 in 2011. Of these new teams, ninety-two percent were directly supported by IPR, which funded personnel costs and the purchase of dogs and equipment.

Since 2002, the Department of Homeland Security (DHS) has provided over $35 billion in funding through homeland security and preparedness grant programs to enhance the capabilities of the nation's emergency responders. These preparedness grants, administered by FEMA's Grant Programs Directorate (GPD), assist states, territories, federally-recognized tribes, local governments, and community-based and private sector stakeholders with forging a unified set of emergency preparedness and response tools.

Preparedness Grants in Action:

- Since 2002, preparedness dollars enabled a 375-percent increase in State and local Urban Search and Rescue (US&R) teams. The tornado that ravaged Joplin, Mo. on May 22, 2011, was responded to by state and local US&R teams. US&R capabilities greatly reduce reliance on federal response efforts and ensure local expertise is leveraged during an incident.
- Over $365 million in preparedness grant dollars helped create a national network of 72 fusion centers, enabling emergency responders to effectively share, interpret and analyze local and national intelligence. After the attempted May 1, 2010 Times Square bombing, fusion centers across the country shared intelligence to support an investigation that resulted in a rapid arrest of the now convicted Times Square Bomber, Faisal Shahzad.
- Preparedness grants provided over $4.6 billion since 2002 to advance interoperable communications, allowing first responders and public service agencies to exchange voice, data and video in real time, facilitating efficient and coordinated response efforts. In 2011, law enforcement officials immediately dispatched a mobile command post to coordinate police, fire, and rescue personnel in response to the barricaded shooter in Marble Falls, Texas.

In 2011, FEMA additionally:

- Established a Program Executive Office (PEO) to coordinate the implementation of *Presidential Policy Directive 8/PPD-8: National Preparedness* with the whole community.
- Trained more than 2.5 million homeland security and emergency management officials and first responders.
- Supported more than 100 exercises in all 56 states and territories to further enhance preparedness and response capabilities. These events included training and exercise planning as well as tabletop, functional and full scale exercises focusing on improvised nuclear device workshops, and hazardous materials.

During a training class at The Center for Domestic Preparedness (CDP) emergency responders including Mayor Richard Hildreth (pictured front-left), of Pacific, Wash., transport a simulated survivor through the initial stage of decontamination. The CDP provides all hazard preparedness training to responders to include Chemical, Biological, Radiological, Nuclear, and Explosive (CBRNE) weapons.

"They really are here to help. We have a lot of confidence in what they will do."

Madison County Commission Chairman Mike Gillespie WHNT-TV Huntsville, Ala. May 4 2011

New York State Emergency Management Office setup a mobile unit in Margretville, N.Y. Margaretville, is one of many rural towns that suffered damage to homes, businesses, roads, and farms by Hurricane Irene.

- The Center for Domestic Preparedness (CDP) completed its biological lab at the Chemical, Ordnance, Biological, and Radiological (COBRA) Training Facility in response to several key homeland security documents calling for specialized training using biological materials. In 2012, responders who complete COBRA courses at the CDP will have had the opportunity to practice proper protection and detection techniques for nerve agents GB and VX and biological materials ricin and anthrax.

- The Chemical Stockpile Emergency Preparedness Program provided grants and technical assistance to support chemical weapons stockpile preparedness in Colorado and Kentucky and transitioned four states and one tribal nation through closeout after 23 years of participation in the program.

- Released the *National Incident Management System (NIMS) Training Program*, the national standardized approach to train and educate emergency responders. FEMA also released the *National Incident Management System (NIMS) Guideline for the Credentialing of Personnel* as the national standard to validate the identity, affiliation, skills, certifications, licensure and authorities of emergency response personnel.

- FEMA's Citizen Corps program registered more than 1,160 state and local Citizen Corps Councils. These Councils were supported by more than 176,000 volunteers throughout the U.S. and its territories, working to prepare and respond to any emergency event in their communities. In total, more than 3 million volunteer hours were recorded.

- Trained over 180,000 federal and non-federal emergency managers nationwide in continuity of operations, devolution, reconstitution, and other continuity-related activities via both resident and independent study courses. This training ensures that our nation's governments at all levels can perform their essential functions during and after a disaster.

A 4th grade class prepares for the Great Central U.S. Shakeout at Milford Elementary School near Atlanta. Representatives from FEMA and the Georgia Emergency Management Agency (GEMA) answer student questions about earthquake preparedness and family emergency preparedness.

FEMA Region 6 staff participates in a video teleconference during the National Level Exercise 11. The meeting took place at the Regional Response Coordination Center (RRCC) Conference Room in Denton Texas.

This tornado siren is a permanent fixture on top of the roof of Monticello, Georgia's city hall. When blasting a warning, the unit swivels 360 degrees, sending a powerful sound throughout the city that can be heard by residents up to two miles away.

FEMA developed and is implementing a National Emergency Management Academy, within the Emergency Management Institute. The Academy's goal is to further professionalize the field of emergency management by providing basic training and education for new emergency managers entering the field. FEMA also published the National Incident Management System Credentialing Guidelines, which provide guidance to ensure disaster-related personnel are properly identified and possess a minimum level of training, experience, physical and medical fitness, and capability appropriate for a particular disaster position.

FEMA also conducted National Level Exercise 2011 which focused on validating catastrophic plans and a whole community response to a major New Madrid Seismic Zone earthquake. As a result of the Secretary's directive to reform the National Exercise Program, FEMA also published the National Exercise Program Base Plan with a focus on smaller-scale, more efficient, limited-notice exercises that are based on validating plans, policies, procedures and lessons learned, which were put into place for Hurricane Irene response efforts.

Integrated Public Alert and Warning System (IPAWS)

IPAWS is America's next-generation infrastructure of alert and warning network, expanding and improving upon traditional audio-only radio and television Emergency Alert System (EAS), delivering emergency alerts to cellular phones through the Commercial Mobile Alert System (CMAS) and integrating with NOAA's National Weather System All Hazards Radio. IPAWS provides support of presidential alerting and warning requirements and use by state, local, tribal and territorial governments, the capability to transmit one alert message over more media to more people.

In 2011, the program accomplished the following:

- Added seven new Primary Entry Point stations to the national emergency alert system, increasing the population of American citizens directly covered by a FEMA-connected radio transmission station to 84 percent.
- Deployed the federal alert aggregator/gateway that serves as the interface enabling authenticated public safety officials to send alerts to multiple public communications systems, including the EAS (radio and TV media), the Commercial Mobile Alerting System (wireless mobile devices), and NOAA National Weather Radio network.
- Conducted the first-ever nationwide test of the EAS. This test helped to identify areas of the existing EAS that need improvement, and helped educate the public safety community and American citizens on the readiness of the EAS.
- Assisted the New York City Office of Emergency Management to become the first public alerting authority to use IPAWS to send emergency alerts to cellular phones.
- Conducted accessible outreach in American Sign Language and engaged non-profit organizations serving the deaf community to develop awareness of the test.

CASE STUDY:
Environmental Health Specialists Assist Alabama

The severe tornadoes that swept through Alabama on April 27, 2011 destroyed more than 6,000 square miles and claimed 248 lives. With power out and water systems and other public infrastructure destroyed following the storms, environmental health specialists were left with the significant challenge of keeping diseases from spreading as citizens dealt with unrefrigerated foods, waste, unfiltered water, and sewage. Luckily, some of these specialists were ready for the challenge thanks to training they received at the Federal Emergency Management Agency's Center for Domestic Preparedness.

As graduates of the Environmental Health Training in Emergency Response (EHTER) course at the CDP's campus in Anniston, Ala., Tim Hatch, environmental program and logistics director from the Alabama Department of Public Health, and Haskey Bryant, environmental health specialist from the Jefferson County Health Department in Birmingham, both knew how to address the environmental health challenges caused by the tornado.

"During the tornadoes in April normal food inspections were not happening. Every disaster has an environmental health component. In Alabama we had power outages, unsafe drinking water, waste disposal, and several other infrastructure issues that affect environmental health. EHTER forced us to plan and have an environmental strategy before the disaster. EHTER provided us a foundation and made our disaster response better," Hayes said

Hatch and Bryant are among a group of more than 50 state and local officials from Alabama who have attended EHTER training at CDP. Since offering the course in 2009, more than 1,170 professionals from across the nation have taken the EHTER course in Anniston. "Environmental health has the components of the food we eat to the water we drink, and we want to make sure that our citizens don't have an increased chance of disease transmission after a disaster," Hatch said

Tim Hatch, Environmental Program and Logistics Director, Montgomery, Ala.

Haskey Bryant, Environmental Health Specialist, Birmingham, Ala.

FIMA manages the National Flood Insurance Program (NFIP) and a range of programs designed to reduce future losses to homes, businesses, schools, public buildings, and critical facilities from floods, earthquakes, hurricanes, tornadoes, and other natural disasters.

Federal Insurance and Mitigation (FIMA)

Mitigating disaster damage and insuring against potential flood damage are essential ingredients of ensuring communities are resilient, sustainable and healthy. By encouraging and supporting disaster mitigation efforts, FEMA leads the nation in reducing the impact of disasters and helping to break the "damage-rebuild-damage" cycle in America's most vulnerable communities. While FIMA serves the lead role in strengthening communities' resilience to disasters through risk analysis, risk reduction, and risk insurance, the whole community – local, state, tribal and territorial governments, academia, businesses, even private citizens – plays a role in ensuring long-term disaster resilience. FEMA recognizes that effective mitigation is incorporated throughout the emergency management cycle; risk analysis informs disaster response and successful disaster recovery builds community resiliency to future disasters.

Hazard mitigation and flood plain management programs save money. Research has shown that every dollar invested in mitigation saves the nation an average of four dollars. Mitigation programs save the American public an estimated $3.4 billion dollars annually through a strategic approach to natural hazard risk management. In 2011, FEMA helped thousands of communities and tens of thousands of individuals avoid the economic loss and human suffering associated with disaster damage, through risk identification and analysis; sound floodplain management strategies; support for stronger building codes; grants to strengthen the built environment; the availability of flood insurance; and responsible environmental planning and historic preservation.

FEMA regions work hand-in-hand with state, local, tribal and territorial governments to ensure the whole community invests in and benefits from mitigation efforts.

"The guys who drew up the FEMA flood maps were brilliant because this is the course where the water flooded. We're all safe and that's the important thing"

Homeowner Joe Floretine,
Asbury Park (NJ) Press
August 30, 2011

Federal Coordinating Officer Sandy Coachman listens to a briefing from Angela Kucherenko, Mitigation Manager, and John Christenson, Public Assistance Manager, on the status of the nine tribal nations that were included in the federal disaster declaration this winter as a result of a severe winter storm.

FIMA manages the National Flood Insurance Program (NFIP) and a range of programs designed to reduce future losses to homes, businesses, schools, public buildings, and critical facilities from floods, earthquakes, tornadoes, and other natural disasters. The Office of Environmental Planning & Historic Preservation is also located within FIMA and provides management and oversight to all FEMA programs in their compliance with environmental planning and historic preservation laws, executive orders and regulations.

National Flood Insurance Program 2011 accomplishments include:

- Wrote 5.5 million flood insurance policies, collected $3.4 billion in written premiums, and financially protected more than $1.2 trillion in property from the devastating effects of floods.
- Reduced subsidies to pre-Flood Insurance Rate Map properties to 21.5 percent, reduced improper claims payments to 1.21 percent, and expanded program management and oversight of the 92 Write-Your-Own insurance companies that sell and service NFIP policies including the thousands of insurance agents and claims adjusters who deliver the insurance program to individual customers.
- Increased participation in the NFIP Community Rating System with the addition of 33 new communities, bringing the total number to 1,164. More than 93 percent of communities receiving new FIRMs adopted the maps by the effective date, thus avoiding suspension from NFIP.
- Paid $1,430,672,460 in flood claims to help citizens recover from flood events. For these claims, FIMA made a payment within an average of 45 days from the reported loss.
- Risk Mapping, Assessment, and Planning (Risk MAP) program helped to strengthen state, local, tribal and territorial government capability by providing actionable risk information, mitigation planning tools, and risk communication outreach support.

Risk MAP 2011 accomplishments include:

- Initiated an additional 385 Risk MAP projects affecting 5,100 communities. Risk Map has now been deployed to watersheds that account for 40% of the U.S. population – well on its way toward its final goal of ensuring that 93 percent of America's population has up-to-date and actionable information on their flood risk.
- Maintained local officials' flood risk awareness at 68 percent in communities where Risk MAP has been deployed.
- Increased the percent of available flood hazard data that meet new, valid, or updated engineering standards to 51 percent and increased the percent of flood hazard data available or in work meeting these standards to 60 percent.

Alabama residents emerge from their safe room moments after an EF-5 tornado demolished their Athens, Ala., home on April 27, 2011. The owners constructed the safe room, using FEMA guidance, in the family garage when they moved into their home. It was the only part of their home to survive the storm.

"We had just come out of the (safe) room and we looked around at what was left, and it was nothing. We were grateful for our lives. If it hadn't been there, we would've been gone."

"You heard the wind like a train and then boom-boom-boom as the walls were falling down. Your ears are popping, and then it's over....It was fast, but it felt like it took forever."

Sarabeth Harrison
Athens, Ala., to CNN's John King

In 2011, Unified Hazard Mitigation Assistance (UHMA) programs helped local communities across the United States prepare for future disasters by providing up to $252 million in flood grant funds for mitigation activities affecting more than 1,300 properties. These measures resulted in losses avoided of approximately $502 million for flood programs.

In addition, the Hazard Mitigation Grant Program obligated approximately $432 million in disaster assistance funds to help communities rebuild stronger and more resiliently after a disaster.

Unified Hazard Mitigation Assistance 2011 accomplishments include:

- Developed an expedited safe room application and approval process.
- Developed the Application Review Tool to assist regions and applicants with the application requirements for acquisition, elevation, mitigation reconstruction, wildfire, safe-room, drainage, and seismic retrofit.
- Developed an enhanced portfolio approach to assist state, local, tribal, and territorial governments that will facilitate a more efficient grant award process.

Other mitigation programs 2011 accomplishments include:

- An increase of over 1,000 jurisdictions in earthquake, flood, or hurricane-prone regions adopt disaster-resistant building codes; currently over 48% of at-risk communities having a disaster-resistant code.
- Supported Shake Out earthquake preparedness drills conducted in California, British Columbia and the Central U.S. including Tennessee, Kentucky, Alabama, Illinois, Missouri, Mississippi, Ohio and Oklahoma.
- Documented a number of success stories of FEMA-funded safe rooms being used to save lives during the 2011 southeast tornado outbreaks.

This elevated home in Hickory Point, N.C. shown here in the background received minor damage during Hurricane Irene, while the home in the foreground was destroyed by over five feet of storm surge. The Carolina Coast was also buffeted by wind gusts in excess of 110 miles per hour.

Sound mitigation efforts helped many homes along the Carolina Coast survive the hurricane and allowed residents to quickly return to their homes.

CASE STUDY:
Floodwall Protected Hospital during Tropical Storm Lee

A floodwall, built with mitigation funds from the Federal Emergency Management Agency (FEMA) and New York State, protected this vital property from 2011 floodwaters. The flood devastated other parts of the city, even as rising water from the Susquehanna River engulfed the hospital's parking lot during Tropical Storm Lee. City officials estimated that as many as 2,000 buildings suffered flood damage from the storm.

Hazard Mitigation might be an inelegant term, but it works. Just ask the folks at Binghamton's Our Lady of Lourdes Hospital.

The hospital, located in the picturesque city of Binghamton, NY with a population of 47,376, and surrounded by rolling hills and rivers, averted major storm damage thanks to hazard mitigation and its floodwall.

When the Susquehanna River flooded in June 2006, the hospital suffered more than $20 million in losses. Floodwater breached an earthen dam, flooding the facility, and critical operations were shut down for 2 weeks. Patients were evacuated and relocated to two other area hospitals. Between 16 to 20 inches of contaminated floodwater covered the hospital's entire ground floor, and the power plant and many essential components sustained severe damage.

After the June 2006 flood, many options were considered including relocation. Using hazard mitigation concepts, procedures and best practices it was determined that constructing a flood wall was the most cost effective. Damage was repaired and a floodwall was built over a five-year period at a cost of approximately $7 million. It was completed in June 2011.

The reinforced concrete floodwall extends 1,365 feet around the hospital between the parking lots and main rear entrance, and reaches heights of 14 feet. It has 10 control gates, which can be operated electronically or manually and accommodates both vehicle and foot traffic.

During Tropical Storm Lee, the hospital staff implemented its emergency plan and had time to manually close all 10 gates. The hospital operated at full capacity during and after the storm. Patients were not evacuated, although there was a contingency plan to do so in an emergency. Only elective surgeries were cancelled and a few services were shut down.

As an entity of DHS - FEMA, the mission of the USFA is to provide national leadership to foster a solid foundation for our fire and emergency services stakeholders in prevention, preparedness, and response.

United States Fire Administration (USFA)

Due to the combined efforts of USFA and its stakeholders, fire-related deaths in the general population have declined by 18.6 percent in the last 10 years (2001-2010). In addition, the number of on-duty firefighter fatalities, excluding the events of Sept. 11, 2001, and the Hometown Heroes' fatalities, has decreased 26 percent.

During 2011, the National Fire Academy (NFA):

- Trained more than 110,000 students representing all 50 states.
- Increased the number of students receiving technology-based distance learning program by 13 percent over the 2010 levels.
- Based on NFA's course evaluation, 89.6 percent of supervisors of students who attended training indicated the information gained helped improve the performance of their departments.
- Improved effectiveness and portability by migrating graphic simulation tools to a commercial off-the-shelf operating system.
- Produced 12 new courses and rewrote 14 existing courses, six of which addressed the 2008 Reauthorization calling for expanded training in Emergency Medical Services.

The National Fire Incident Reporting System (NFIRS) modernization and enhancement efforts focused on improved flexibility and efficiency in access to data warehousing and mining. Internal FEMA customers began the initial testing of the improved NFIRS.

Improvement to the National Emergency Training Center (NETC) facility continued with establishing 100 percent emergency power to all facility structures, the completion of the installation of the geothermal heating/air conditioning in four buildings, and awarding contracts to install a natural gas line to supply gas for new boilers in 11 buildings. This will eliminate the dependency on a neighboring steam plant for heat and hot water and ultimately will reduce cost and carbon emissions. USFA also updated and drafted new campus security procedures to enhance student and employee safety.

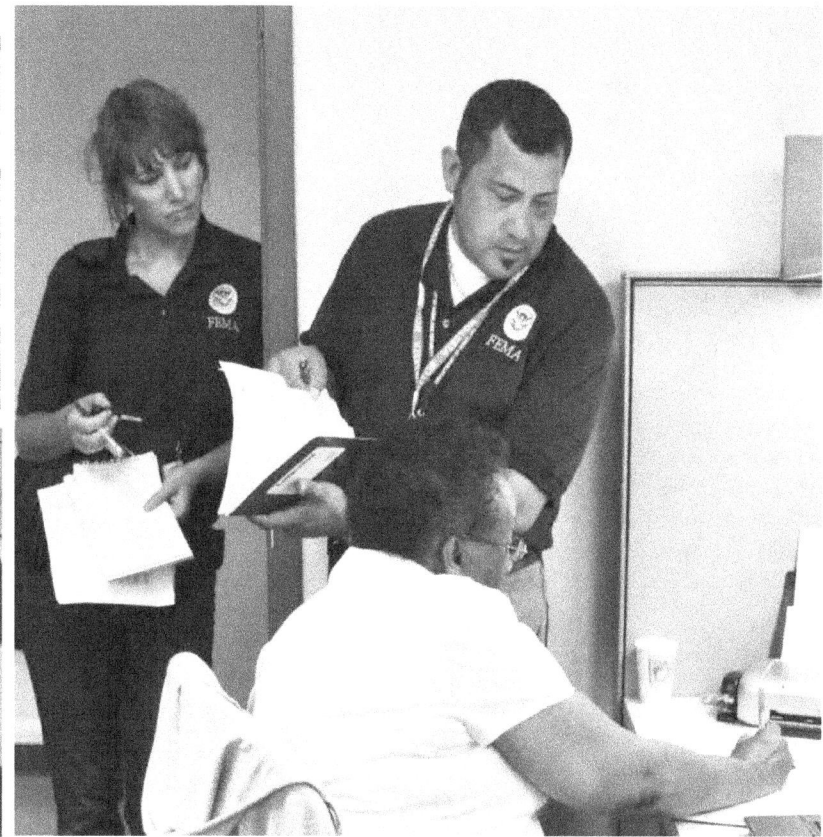

Provide *Timely, Positive, Accountable, and Dependable* support, tools, and resources FEMA needs to build, sustain and improve our capability to prepare for, protect against, respond to, recover from, and mitigate against all hazards.

Mission Support Bureau

The Mission Support Bureau (MSB) supports all facets of the agency mission by providing strategic leadership to and assuring the timely, efficient, and effective delivery of administrative, property management, health and safety, human capital, information technology, procurement, security services and business function capabilities.

The Mission Support Bureau delivers vital services and support that constitute the essential backbone to accomplish FEMA's mission. When viewed as an integrated whole, the products, resources, and services the Bureau delivers are the very foundation—the brick and mortar—upon which every staff and program office can build success.

Region 5 FEMA Community Relations representative shows a local resident in Ottawa, Ohio, the look of the proper FEMA credentials. During disaster recovery, affected residents must be on the lookout for possible fraud.

Region 2 FEMA employees at the Joint Field Office in Colonie, N.Y. take part in an evacuation drill.

Equal Rights Specialist James E. Parker leads a training session for FEMA workers deployed to Joplin, Mo. The Equal Rights Trilogy of classes is mandatory for all FEMA workers on a yearly basis. This and other in-field training supports FEMA's goals by improving the competencies of specialists to prevent, prepare for, respond to, recover from, and mitigate the potential effects of all types of disasters and emergencies on the American people.

In 2011, MSB accomplished the following:

- Recouped $339 million through aggressive deobligation of unused contract funds.
- Identified 681 potential fraud cases by the Office of the Chief Security Officer Fraud Prevention and Investigation Branch, of which 57 percent were referred for recovery of funds resulting in $3.27 million recovered.
- Invested $20.4 million to perform repairs at agency facilities through 206 separate projects to maintain their mission capability, eliminate life safety issues, and replace obsolete building systems.
- Significantly reduced the pending Freedom of Information Act backlogs. In 2011, 820 new cases were received and 1,139 cases were closed, which reduced the number of backlogged cases from 710 to 453.
- Established new orientation and new-hire programs. Trained 330 new hires in residence in a new four-day training course at the National Emergency Training Center (NETC) in Emmitsburg, MD. The course orients new FEMA employees about the agency, its mission, its culture, and how to work across the organization. Trained 146 new hires in the new two-day on-boarding program. New employees now report to work to a fully equipped functional work area with access to the full suite of employee tools (email, voicemail, time and attendance system, travel system, etc.).
- Established an Industry Liaison Local Business Transition Team to facilitate the transition of disaster requirements/contracts to local businesses within the disaster area and to coordinate business outreach activities with Joint Field Office staff and the private sector.
- Stood up the Disaster Acquisition Response Team for regional deployment, which will focus on achieving efficiencies in administering and closing out disaster contracts.
- The Regional Disability Integration Specialists and deployed Equal Rights Officers provided training to deployed JFO staff about disability issues and legal requirements pertaining to people with disabilities and those with access and functional needs.
- Provided fraud awareness and prevention training to more than 1000 Agency employees in compliance with the Post Katrina Emergency Management Reform Act.
- Established a Suspicious Activity Reporting System as part of DHS's nationwide program for reporting suspicious behavior to detect, deter and prevent terrorists' activities on FEMA controlled property or assets.
- Developed and implemented a plan to reduce collection of Social Security Numbers associated with five FEMA Learning Management Systems by 99% by July 2012. Increased privacy awareness training – evident in trends showing a correlation in the reduction of privacy incidents; reduced vulnerabilities in FEMA programs and systems; better privacy practices of the workforce; and, decreased dollars spent to remediate incidents.
- Acquisitions researched 3,453 contracts to search for opportunities to de-obligate funds, resulting in successful de-obligation of more than $284 million dollars as a result of proper contracting administrative techniques and close-out procedures.

Section III

2013
Budget in Brief

"Our communication with the federal government has been good." (In response to Hurricane Irene in New Jersey.)

New Jersey Governor
Chris Christie
Good Morning America
August 28, 2011

The North Carolina Baptist Men Disaster Relief Organization set up their base in Bayboro, N.C. Voluntary agencies work closely with FEMA to identify those in need of assistance which volunteers can provide.

2013 Budget in Brief Overview

Ensuring Resilience to Disasters

State and Local Grants: The 2013 request sustains federal funding for state and local preparedness grants totaling $2.9 billion, highlighting the Department's commitment to moving resources out of Washington, D.C. and into the hands of state and local first responders who are often best positioned to detect and respond to terrorism, other threats, and natural disasters.

Disaster Relief Fund (DRF): $6.1 billion is requested for the DRF to allow FEMA to continue to address the impacts of a disaster on individuals and communities across the nation. The DRF provides a significant portion of the total federal response to victims in presidentially declared disasters or emergencies.

	FY 2011 Cont. Resolution[1]		FY 2012	Enacted	FY 2013 Pres. Budget		FY 2013 +/- FY 2012	
	FTE	$000	FTE	$000	FTE	$000	FTE	$000
Salaries and Expenses [1,2]	3,822	$1,068,585 [3]	4,271	$1,031,378 [4]	3,576	789,172	(695)	(242,206)
State and Local Programs	0 [6]	2,103,039[3]	85 [6]	1,265,403 [4]	876	2,900,212	791	1,634,809
Emergency Management Performance Grants	15	339,320	15	339,500	[7]	[7]	(15)	(339,500)
Assistance to Firefighter Grants	0	761,494[3]	81	641,250[4]	[7]	[7]	(81)	(641,250)
United States Fire Administration	115	45,497	148	44,038	159	42,520	11	(1,518)
Collections – Radiological Emergency Preparedness Program	158	(265)	196	(896)	194	(1,443)	(2)	(547)
Disaster Relief Fund [8]	5,645	2,523,343[3]	4,852	7,076,000	4,852	6,088,926	---	(987,074)
Flood Hazard Mapping and Risk Analysis Program	51	181,636	80	97,712	80	89,329	---	(8,383)
Disaster Assistance Direct Loan Program	0	294	0	295	0	0	---	(295)
National Pre-Disaster Mitigation Fund	15	49,900	12	35,500	7	0	(5)	(35,500)
Emergency Food and Shelter	0	119,760	0	120,000	0	100,000	---	(20,000)
Net Discretionary – Excluding Support	9,821	$7, 192,603	9,740	$10,650,180	9,744	$10,008,716	4	($641,164)
National Flood Insurance Fund Discretionary	260	169,000	279	171,000	279	171,000	---	---
National Flood Insurance Fund Mandatory	29	3,085,000	29	3,102,748	29	3,380,000	---	277,252
Subtotal	10,110	$10,446,603	10,048	13,923,928	10,052	13,559,716	4	(364,212)
Total Budget Authority	10,110	$10,446,603	10,048	13,923,928	10,052	13,559,716	4	(364,212)
Less prior year Rescissions	0	(30,986)[9]	0	(4,016) [10]	0	0	0	0

[1] The Salaries and Expenses appropriation was named "Management and Administration" prior to FY 2012.

[2] Pursuant to P.L. 112-103, the amount for Management and Administration (M&A) in FY 2011 includes 862 FTE funded by the transfer from the Disaster Relief Fund (DRF).

[3] Pursuant to P.L. 112-103, transfers to the M&A (now Salaries and Expenses) appropriation in FY 2011 include: $129.487 million from State and Local Programs (SALP), $46.886 million from Firefighter Assistance Grants (AFG), and $105.389 million from DRF. The amounts shown for these appropriations reflect the transfers.

[4] Pursuant to P.L. 112-74, the amount for Salaries and Expenses in FY 2012 includes $91.778 million transferred from SALP. It also include $33.75 million from AFG and $10.5 million from Emergency Management Performance Grants (EMPG) that were not transferred but are shown in SALP for compatibility across the years.

[5] FYs 2011 and 2012 for SALP include funding for National Special Security Events in the amounts of $7.485 million and $7.5 million, respectively.

[6] The FTE amount for SALP is included in the Salaries and Expenses FTE amount for FYs 2011 and 2012. However, FTE for the Emergency Management Institute remains in SALP in FY 2012.

[7] Amounts for EMPG and AFG are included in SALP for FY 2013.

[8] Pursuant to P.L. 112-10, the DRF transferred $15.968 million to the Office of Inspector General in FY 2011, and pursuant to P.L. 112-74, will transfer $24 million in FY 2012. The amounts shown reflect the transfers.

[9] Pursuant to P.L. 112-10, $30.986 million was rescinded in FY 2011 – M&A FY 2010 balances - $814,153; National Pre-disaster Mitigation - $19.603 million; Office of Domestic Preparedness - $10.569 million.

[10] Pursuant to P.L. 112-74, $4.016 million was rescinded in FY 2012 – M&A FY 2011 balances - $216,744; National Pre-disaster Mitigation - $678,213; Office of Domestic Preparedness - $3.121 million.

Elizabeth Harman, FEMA Assistant Administrator for Grant Programs, greets members of Phoenix Fire Department recruit class 11-1 during a break from live fire training held in Region 9 on January 19, 2011. The class of 28 firefighters is funded by a Staffing for Adequate Fire and Emergency Response grant (SAFER).

Vermont National Guard members secure pallets of bottled water aboard a helicopter at FEMA's distribution center at Camp Johnson in Colchester, Vt. FEMA Region 1 provided emergency supplies, including food, water, tarps and other necessary items which the Vermont State Police and National Guard delivered to flooded towns in Vermont.

Firefighters, who were first on the scene when an EF-5 tornado on May 22, 2011 tore a path in Joplin, participated in the opening ceremony of the "I AM JOPLIN" event, a back-to-school gathering attended by thousands of school-aged children and their parents at Missouri Southern State University.

2013 Appropriation Details:

The Department's 2013 budget for FEMA will focus on achieving success in one of DHS' core missions - ensuring domestic response to disasters. The 2013 budget places a strong emphasis on funding the key programs that help to ensure that, as a Nation, we are prepared at the federal, state, local, tribal and territorial levels to effectively and rapidly respond to and recover from a variety of disasters.

State and Local Programs $654.0M

The 2013 President's Budget funds state and local programs at $2.9 billion and proposes a new homeland security grants program to better develop, sustain and leverage core capabilities across the country to support national preparedness and response. The 2013 National Preparedness Grant Program (NPGP) consolidates FEMA's current preparedness grant programs—with the exception of the Emergency Management Performance Grant and Assistance to Firefighter Grants—into a comprehensive preparedness grant program. The NPGP, which supports the core capabilities outlined in the National Preparedness Goal, will focus on creating a robust national response capacity based on cross-jurisdictional and readily deployable state and local assets rather than meeting mandates from multiple individual, and often disconnected, grant programs. Using a competitive, risk-based model, the NPGP will use a comprehensive process for identifying and prioritizing deployable capabilities; limit periods of performance to put funding to work quickly; and require grantees to regularly report progress in the acquisition and development of these capabilities. The increase will also help instill the whole community approach by empowering state and local programs with the tools and training required to support an effective emergency management operation.

2013 Major Program Decreases:

Disaster Relief Fund (DRF)   -$987.0M

The 2013 President's Budget provides $6.088.9 billion for the DRF. Through the DRF, FEMA provides a significant portion of the total federal response to presidentially declared major disasters and emergencies. The request funds the projected needs of the DRF in accordance with the methodology of the Budget Control Act (BEA) of 2012, of which $607.9 million is funded from FEMA's base budget. The funding level required for the catastrophic category (events greater than $500 million) is based on FEMA spend plans for all previously declared catastrophic events and is projected to be approximately $1 billion less in 2013 than required in 2012. The request includes no funds for new catastrophic events that may occur in 2013 and assumes that these will be funded with emergency supplemental funding as provided for in the BCA. The non-catastrophic funding level is based on a revised approach that uses the ten-year average for noncatastrophic events. As opposed to the previous method that utilized the five-year average, this provides a more accurate projection of noncatastrophic needs since it normalizes the effects of outlier years.

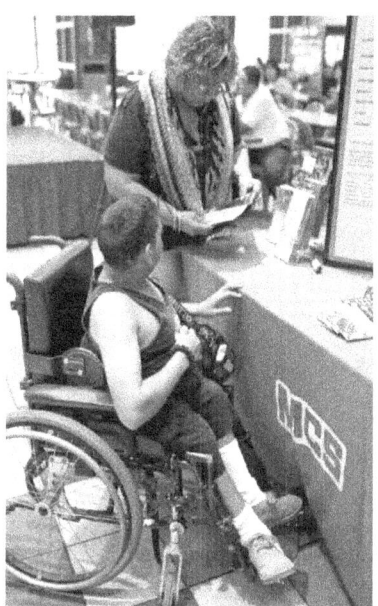

A Region 2 National Flood Insurance Program Specialist provides information about the program to a disaster survivor at an outreach event in Vega Alta, P.R.

Salary and Expenses   -$242.2M

The 2013 President's Budget funds salary and expenses at $781.9 million. The Department is committed to improving efficiency by streamlining current business processes and harnessing the use of innovative technologies while ensuring the Nation's resilience from disasters. Approximately $61 million of the reduction represents the elimination of one-time funding initiatives and the net of program decreases such as the elimination of Primary Entry Point (PEP), rent reductions and other management efficiencies. The administration of state and local programs, partially funded in the salary and expenses appropriation in 2012, is now funded entirely within the state and local programs appropriation in 2013.

Emergency Food and Shelter   -$20.0M

The budget provides $100 million for the Emergency Food and Shelter program, consistent with previous Administration budget requests. This funding level reflects an agency-wide focus on FEMA's primary mission of preparing for and coordinating disaster response and recovery efforts while still providing substantial support for this non-disaster program. This request will continue to supplement the delivery of an estimated 46.5 million meals, 3.1 million nights of lodging, and support for 74,706 rent/mortgage payments and 155,567 utility bill payments across the nation.

Pre-disaster Mitigation   -$35.5M

The 2013 budget includes no new funding for pre-disaster mitigation due to continuing large unobligated balances which will finance both grant-making and administrative expenses in 2013. Additionally, mitigation projects and hazard mitigation plans are eligible for funding in other FEMA grant programs.

Flood Hazard Mapping and Risk Analysis   -$8.4M

The 2013 amount of $89.4 million reflects the austere budget proposed where hard decisions needed to be made about what to sustain. This critical program remains funded, along with the additional funds derived from the NFIP, at a level that can sustain the program with outcomes achieved over a longer duration.

Diana Kidder, Region 1 National Flood Insurance Program Specialist, speaks to local residents in Plainville, Conn. after a town meeting to discuss programs available from federal, state and local partners if impacted by Tropical Storm Irene.

Businesses inundated with water in the Oak Park neighborhood near the Souris River in Minot, N.D. FEMA provided assistance to disaster survivors in Ward and Burleigh counties.

In the days and weeks that followed the Joplin, Mo. tornado, FEMA Disability Integration Specialists, forged a direct partnership with Joplin's Independent Living Center to help ensure survivors with disabilities had their most urgent needs met as quickly as possible.

The Bond Creek North Carolina neighborhood was hit hard and is recovering from the damages done by Hurricane Irene. FEMA Region 4 is helping individuals recover from the storm with grants and where needed, temporary housing.

A professional engineer in FEMA's Region 1 Office of Risk Analysis Branch of the Mitigation Division, leads a class for more than 60 local officials during a National Flood Insurance Program Workshop in Old Lyme, Conn.

2013 Major Program, Limited to No Funding Changes:
Dollars in thousands.

Emergency Management Performance Grants
Enacted, 2011	$ 339,320
Appropriation, 2012	$ 339,500
Budget Estimate, 2013 (Included in SALP)	

Assistance to Firefighters Grants
Enacted, 2011	$ 761,494
Appropriation, 2012	$ 641.250
Budget Estimate, 2013 (Included in SALP)	

United States Fire Administration
Enacted, 2011	$ 45,497
Appropriation, 2012	$ 44,038
Budget Estimate, 2013	$ 42,520

Collections – Radiological Emergency Preparedness Program
Enacted, 2011	$ -265
Appropriation, 2012	$ -896
Budget Estimate, 2013	-$ 1,443

Disaster Assistance Direct Loan Program
Enacted, 2011	$ 294
Appropriation, 2012	$ 295
Budget Estimate, 2013 – no funding requested.	

National Flood Insurance Fund Discretionary
Enacted, 2011	$ 169,000
Appropriation, 2012	$ 171,000
Budget Estimate, 2013	$ 171,000

National Flood Insurance Fund Mandatory
Enacted, 2011	$ 3,085,000
Appropriation, 2012	$ 3,102,748
Budget Estimate, 2013	$ 3,380,000

Section IV

FEMA Statistics and Figures

"There should be no such complaints about how the Obama Administration and FEMA responded to the severe storms and killer tornadoes that struck across the South, especially Alabama...Clearly, Fugate and the Obama Administration get it."

Columnist Joey Kennedy
Birmingham News
May 4, 2011.

2011-2012 FEMA Statistics and Figures

Prior to the tornado that hit Tuscaloosa, Ala. on April 27, 2011, Mayor Walter Maddox and 66 of his staff used preparedness grant funds to attend training at the Emergency Management Institute. He later told the *New York Times* that the training had "done more to help Tuscaloosa handle the disaster than anything else."

Since 2002, over 16.5 million training events supported by FEMA preparedness grants have increased first responders' preparedness capabilities.

- 13 Preparedness Grants were awarded to 56 states, territories, District of Columbia and federally recognized tribes, totaling over $2.3 billion dollars.

- Emergency Management Institute (EMI) Training by the Numbers:
  - More than 5.5 million active students
  - 30,559 classroom course completions (This represents a 26% increase from 2010)
  - 2,275,174 Independent Study Program online course completions. (This represents a 16% increase from 2010)

- EMI hosted three national-level conferences:
  - National Training and Exercise Conference
  - Emergency Management Higher Education Conference
  - National Dam Safety Program Technical Seminar

- FEMA's Higher Education Program has resulted in the following 253 collegiate emergency management degree programs:

  - 232 collegiate emergency management programs.
  - 68 certificate, diploma, focus-area, minor in Emergency Management collegiate programs.
  - 46 schools offer associate degree programs.
  - 43 schools offer bachelor degree programs.
  - 86 schools with master-level concentrations/tracks/specializations/ emphasis areas/degrees
  - Ten schools offer doctoral-level programs.

- The National Training and Education Division facilitated training for 209,630 first responders in 2011.

- FEMA's all-hazards Center for Domestic Preparedness (CDP) trained 93,560 local, state, tribal and territorial responders from across the U.S. in preventing and responding to disasters and other terrorist threats involving chemical, biological, radiological, nuclear and explosive materials.

- CDP also provided mobile training support to local jurisdictions leading to five 2012 National Special Security Events:

  - Democratic National Convention
  - Republican National Convention
  - Asian Pacific Economic Cooperation (APEC) Summit
  - G8 Summit
  - NATO Summit

Donald Waters, 2011 FEMA Combined Federal Campaign National Capital Region Manager, speaks with FEMA employees about the campaign. Each year, the CFC raises millions of dollars to donate to charities and philanthropic organizations across the U.S.

A responder surveys a simulated accident scene to quickly assess and triage potential survivors during training at the Center for Domestic Preparedness (CDP) in Anniston, Ala. The CDP recently incorporated a school bus into training scenarios at the Chemical, Ordnance, Biological, and Radiological Training Facility.

Region 8 FEMA Community Relations employee talks to a flood survivor. FEMA is supporting the emergency management team in providing disaster assistance to those affected by the flooding.

- USFA National Fire Academy (NFA) by the numbers:

  - 6,662 students trained in residence at Emmitsburg.
  - 5,243 students trained in off campus classrooms with / through our state partners.
  - 47,159 completed independent study *NFA*Online courses.
  - 51,048 students received NFA classroom training through training in partnership with accredited State Fire Training systems / instructors.
    - These classes are financed by a $26K grant given to each State Training System. Each State accounts for the $26K grant by submitting the short-form application for each student they train.

- USFA hosted five national-level conferences:

  - The Executive Fire Officer Symposium (graduates of the EFO program research symposium).
  - Training, Resources and Data Exchange (TRADE) Conference – consists of the 150 largest metro fire departments and the 50 State Fire Training System.
  - Prevention, Advocacy and Data Exchange (PARADE) –consists of the 50 State Fire Marshals and local fire marshals.
  - The National Fire Information Council - National Fire Incident Reporting System conference.
  - Fire and Emergency Services Higher Education (FESHE) conference.

- Mission Support Bureau Statistics and Figures:

  - Reduced the Agency Scope 1 & 2 Greenhouse Gas Emissions by 2%.
  - Brought 90 of regulated tanks into OSHE compliance in 2011 = 24%.
  - Increased by 10% the number of employees on formal individual development plans in order to identify training and development opportunities to improve an employee's skills and knowledge to support agency's mission.
  - Processed 95% of training authorization forms within five business days and remaining 5% averaging no more than ten business days, resulting in timely delivery of training to employees.
  - Identified 681 potential fraud cases by the Office of the Chief Security Officer Fraud Prevention and Investigation Branch, of which 57 percent were referred for recovery of funds resulting in $3.27 million recovered.
  - Office of the Chief Security Officer, Fraud & Internal Investigations Division, identified $3.38 million for recovery of suspected fraud or improper disaster assistance payments. From October 1, 2012 to date, Office of the Chief Security Officer has prevented the disbursement of, or recommended recoupment of over $1.22 million of fraudulent or improper disaster assistance payments.